IMPACTING EARTH
HOW PEOPLE CHANGE THE LAND

CONSTRUCTING TOWNS AND CITIES

AMY GREENAN

PowerKiDS press
New York

Published in 2019 by The Rosen Publishing Group, Inc.
29 East 21st Street, New York, NY 10010

First Edition

Editor: Jennifer Lombardo
Book Design: Tanya Dellaccio

Photo Credits: Cover TierneyMJ/Shutterstock.com; p. 5 stockelements/Shutterstock.com; p. 7 nesrin ozdemir/Shutterstock.com; p. 9 Boris Stroujko/Shutterstock.com; p. 11 Srijaroen/Shutterstock.com; p. 13 (main) Rawpixel.com/Shutterstock.com; p. 13 (inset) Rokas Tenys/Shutterstock.com; p. 14 GeorginaCaptures/Shutterstock.com; p. 15 AsiaTravel/Shutterstock.com; p. 17 Antonio Guillem/ Shutterstock.com; p. 19 Maaskot/Getty Images; p. 21 TTstudio/Shutterstock.com; p. 22 Pressmaster/Shutterstock.com.

Library of Congress Cataloging-in-Publication Data

Names: Greenan, Amy, author.
Title: Constructing towns and cities / Amy Greenan.
Description: New York : PowerKids Press, [2019] | Series: Impacting Earth : how people change the land | Includes bibliographical references and index.
Identifiers: LCCN 2018028658| ISBN 9781538341872 (library bound) | ISBN 9781538341858 (pbk.) | ISBN 9781538341865 (6 pack)
Subjects: LCSH: City planning–Juvenile literature. | Urban pollution–Juvenile literature. | Urban ecology (Sociology)–Juvenile literature.
Classification: LCC TD160 .G74 2019 | DDC 307.1/416–dc23
LC record available at https://lccn.loc.gov/2018028658

CPSIA Compliance Information: Batch #CWPK19. For Further Information contact Rosen Publishing, New York, New York at 1-800-237-9932

CONTENTS

THINKING ABOUT THE ENVIRONMENT

When people live close together in cities or towns, they can share things with each other that make their lives easier. However, these bigger communities can also hurt our **environment**. Today, people are learning about ways to make living in cities good for Earth and figuring out how we can live in ways that are both safe and easy.

KNOW YOUR ZONE

SETTLING DOWN

People used to move from place to place. After many years, they began to settle down into small groups of **dwellings** called villages. By living near each other, people could help each other in different ways. They could hunt together for food or watch each other's children. They helped guard the village, too.

IT TOOK A WHILE

Over 11,000 years ago, people formed the first villages. It took another 5,000 years for large cities to appear!

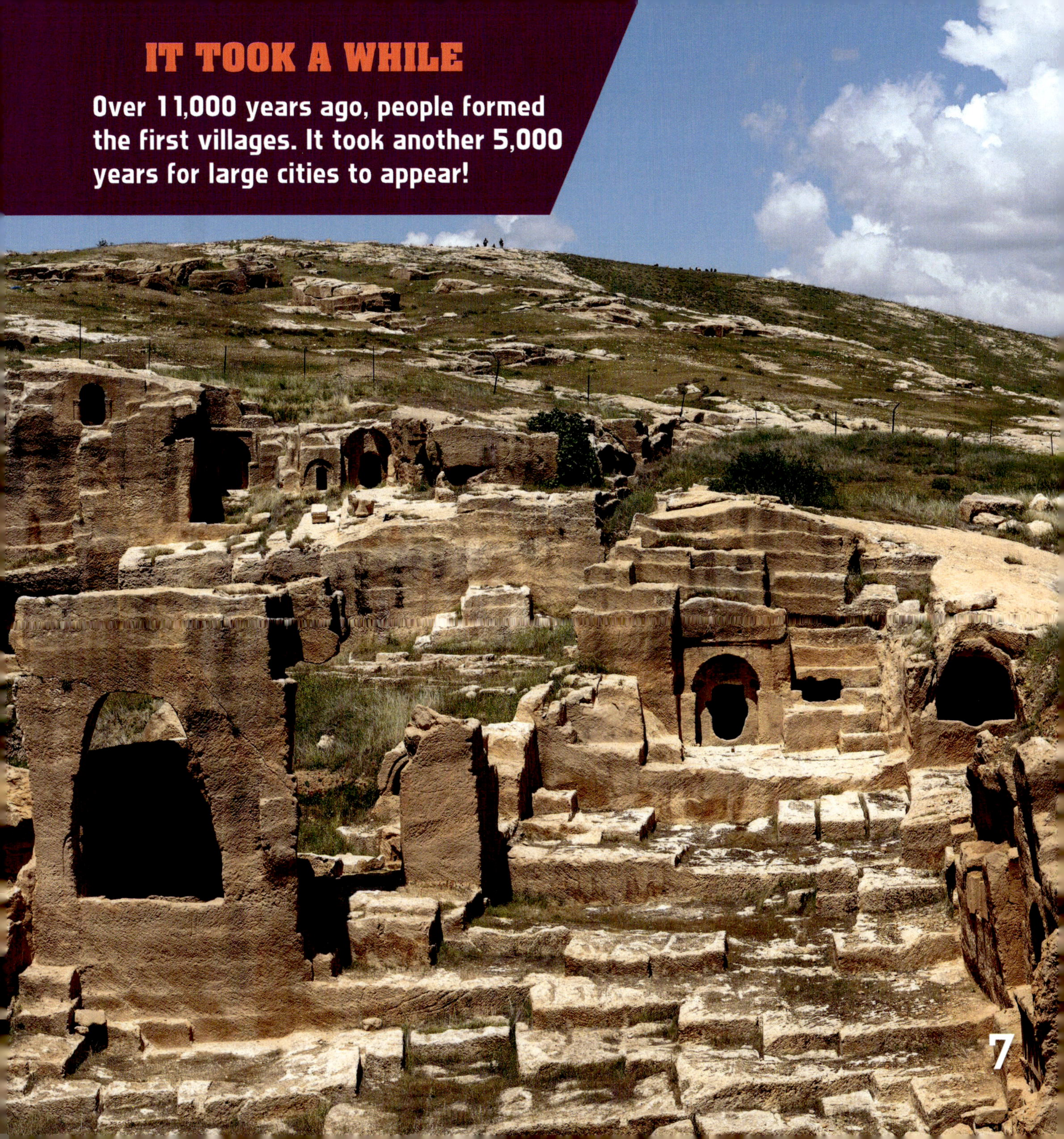

WE ARE NOT ALONE

When people build a town or city, it changes the environment. The buildings and roads people make may take away natural parts of the land, such as mountains and rivers. There isn't enough room for all the animals and plants that lived there before. The plants die and the animals have to move to a new place.

TAKING OVER

Humans are the most **invasive** animals on Earth. Our numbers could grow to almost 10 billion by 2050!

BAD THINGS FOR THE ENVIRONMENT

People can be messy! Sometimes we don't think about how the things we do every day might be bad for the environment. It's important that people get rid of waste and trash in the right ways. If waste and trash get into people's drinking water or are thrown away too close to people's houses, they can make people and animals sick.

HOW WE CAN DO BETTER

Today, many towns and cities make plans to be sure they're not hurting the land and wildlife. Recycling is one way to make sure we won't run out of things we need. For example, paper is made out of trees, but new paper can also be made out of old paper so we don't have to cut down more trees. This also leaves more forests for us to enjoy.

CITIES AND TOWNS TOMORROW

People are building new cities and towns even today! Builders work with architects—people who plan buildings. Today, architects try to make buildings that save **energy** and help the environment. Creating an environmentally friendly city from the start is important. Having nature and a city's buildings safely side by side is good for everyone.

JAKARTA, INDONESIA

MANY NEW CITIES

Many countries around the world are building new cities. In Indonesia, almost 30 new cities are being built today!

JAKARTA, INDONESIA

TECHNOLOGY IN THE CITY

The tools we use to deal with problems can help our lives in many ways. These tools can help a city or town work better for the people who live there. Phone **apps** can let people share their thoughts about how the city can be better or help plan public spaces in ways that don't change the land too much.

THAT'S A LOT!

By 2050, more than 60 percent of the world's people might live in cities.

SAVING ENERGY IN CITIES

Some parts of city life can be good for the environment. For example, city homes are mostly smaller spaces that don't use as much energy as big houses. Using less energy helps stop the planet from getting too warm. When Earth warms up too much, the **climate** starts to change, which makes life hard for the plants and animals in many areas.

DO YOUR PART

People who live in towns and cities can keep making things better for Earth in small ways. You can recycle paper and cans when you're done with them, turn off the lights when you leave a room, pick up any trash you find on the ground, and turn off the water when you brush your teeth. People in cities can work together to clean up parks and other public spaces.

MAKE A DIFFERENCE!

The simple act of turning off the lights saves energy. This means you'll use fewer **fossil fuels**.

MAKING LIFE BETTER

There are good things about towns and cities, but they can change the land in harmful ways. Learn as much as you can about how you can live in a cleaner, more environmentally friendly way. Your life will be better, and you'll help make the world a better place for everyone!

GLOSSARY

app (application): A computer program, or set of orders that does a job.

climate: The weather in a place over a long period of time.

dwelling: A place to live.

energy: The power to work or to act.

environment: The natural world around us.

fossil fuel: A fuel—such as coal, oil, or natural gas—that is formed in the earth over millions of years from dead plants or animals.

invasive: Tending to spread quickly in a new area.

INDEX

WEBSITES

Due to the changing nature of Internet links, PowerKids Press has developed an online list of websites related to the subject of this book. This site is updated regularly. Please use this link to access the list:
www.powerkidslinks.com/hpcl/towns